My First Animal Books

ANIMALS ON THE MOVE

Junia K. Johnson

TABLE OF CONTENTS

A Crabtree Seedlings Book

Animals on the Move

The **tiger** runs.

The fish swims.

The **monkey** climbs.

The **kangaroo** hops.

The bird flies.

The snake slithers.

The **turtle** crawls.

The frog jumps.

And I wiggle and play.

So many ways to move!

Glossary

kangaroo (kang-guh-ROO): A kangaroo is an animal that uses its strong back legs to jump. A kangaroo mom carries her baby in her pouch.

monkey (MUHNG-kee): A monkey is an animal that has hands and feet to help it climb. Most monkeys have tails.

tiger (TYE-gur): A tiger is an animal that eats only meat. In the wild, it has to run fast to catch its dinner.

turtle (TUR-tuhl): A turtle is an animal that hatches from an egg. When baby sea turtles hatch, they crawl to the ocean.

Index

School-to-Home Support for Caregivers and Teachers

This book helps children grow by letting them practice reading. Here are a few guiding questions to help the reader build his or her comprehension skills. Possible answers appear here in red.

Before Reading

- **What do I think this book is about?** I think this book is about places where animals go. I think this book is about how animals move.
- **What do I want to learn about this topic?** I want to learn more about animals that have four legs. I want to learn if all animals can move fast.

During Reading

- **I wonder why...** I wonder why monkeys climb trees. I wonder why a turtle crawls slowly.
- **What have I learned so far?** I have learned that a kangaroo and a frog hop. I have learned that snakes slither.

After Reading

- **What details did I learn about this topic?** I have learned that a monkey is an animal that has hands and feet to help it climb. I have learned that a tiger is an animal that eats only meat.
- **Read the book again and look for the glossary words.** I see the word *kangaroo* on page 9, and the word *turtle* on page 14. The other glossary words are found on pages 22 and 23.

Crabtree Publishing

crabtreebooks.com 800-387-7650

In Canada: We acknowledge the financial support of the Government of Canada through the Canada Book Fund for our publishing activities.

Hardcover 978-1-0396-6025-0
Paperback 978-1-0396-6220-9

Printed in Canada
122023/CP20231221

Published in Canada
Crabtree Publishing
616 Welland Avenue
St. Catharines, Ontario
L2M 5V6

Published in the United States
Crabtree Publishing
347 Fifth Avenue
Suite 1402-145
New York, NY 10016

Written by: Junia K. Johnson
Print book version produced jointly with Blue Door Education in 2023

Photo Credits: snake © Ryan M. Bolton, tiger © Nick Biemans, fish © Nicola Gavin, monkey © Sam DCruz, kangaroo © Christopher Meder, bird © nuruddean, turtle © Benjamin Albiach Galan, frog © muhamad mizan bin ngateni, girl © Thomas M Perkins; All images from Shutterstock.com

Library and Archives Canada
Cataloguing in Publication
Available at the Library and Archives Canada

Library of Congress
Cataloging-in-Publication Data
Available at the Library of Congress